THE ART OF SONG

A graded selection of songs
through the ages

Grade 7

high voice

ALLE RECHTE VORBEHALTEN · ALL RIGHTS RESERVED
EDITION PETERS
PUBLISHED BY FABER MUSIC
LEIPZIG · LONDON · NEW YORK

Download accompaniment tracks and practice tracks by scanning the QR code or going to fabermusic.com/editionpetersresources.

Cover images (clockwise from top left): Around the Piano, Firle, Walther (1859–1929) / Waterhouse and Dodd, London, UK, / The Bridgeman Art Library; The Singing Lesson, 1882 (oil on canvas), Toulouse-Lautrec, Henri de (1864–1901) / Musee Toulouse-Lautrec, Albi, France, Lauros / Giraudon / The Bridgeman Art Library; Die Lautenspielerin, Borch d. J., Gerard ter (1617–1681); Schubert at the Piano, 1899 (oil on canvas), Klimt, Gustav (1862–1918); The Love Song, c. 1717 (oil on canvas), Watteau, Jean-Antoine (1684–1721); Les café-concert des Ambassadeurs, 1876/7 (pastel on montype), Degas, Edgar Germain Hilaire (1834–1917)

This edition © Copyright 2008 by Hinrichsen Edition, Peters Edition Limited, London

CONTENTS

Morley	I saw my lady weeping	4
Purcell	What shall I do	6
Purcell	If music be the food of love	8
Rosseter	When Laura smiles	11
Handel	How beautiful are the feet	14
Mozart	Un moto di gioia	16
Handel	But Thou didst not leave His soul in hell	19
Handel	Behold and see if there be any sorrow	22
Purcell	An Epithalamium: Thrice happy lovers	24
Beethoven	Ich liebe dich	28
Brahms	Feldeinsamkeit	30
Brahms	O liebliche Wangen	33
Brahms	Wiegenlied	38
Brahms	Scheiden und Meiden	40
Schubert	An den Frühling	41
Schubert	An den Frühling	42
Schubert	Die Forelle	44
Schubert	Nachtviolen	48
Schubert	Frühlingsglaube	50
Schumann	Mondnacht	53
Schumann	Die Lotosblume	56
Verdi	Il poveretto	58
Tosti	'A vucchella	62
Wolf	Der Musikant	67
Wolf	Der Gärtner	70
German	She had a letter from her love	74
Sullivan	Is life a boon?	77
Sullivan	The sun, whose rays are all ablaze	80

I saw my lady weeping

Anonymous
Thomas Morley (1557–1602)

range:

Edition Peters No. 71768
© Copyright 2008 by Hinrichsen Edition, Peters Edition Ltd, London

range:

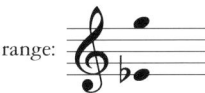

What shall I do

from *Dioclesian*

Thomas Betterton (*c.*1635–1710)

Henry Purcell (1659–1695)

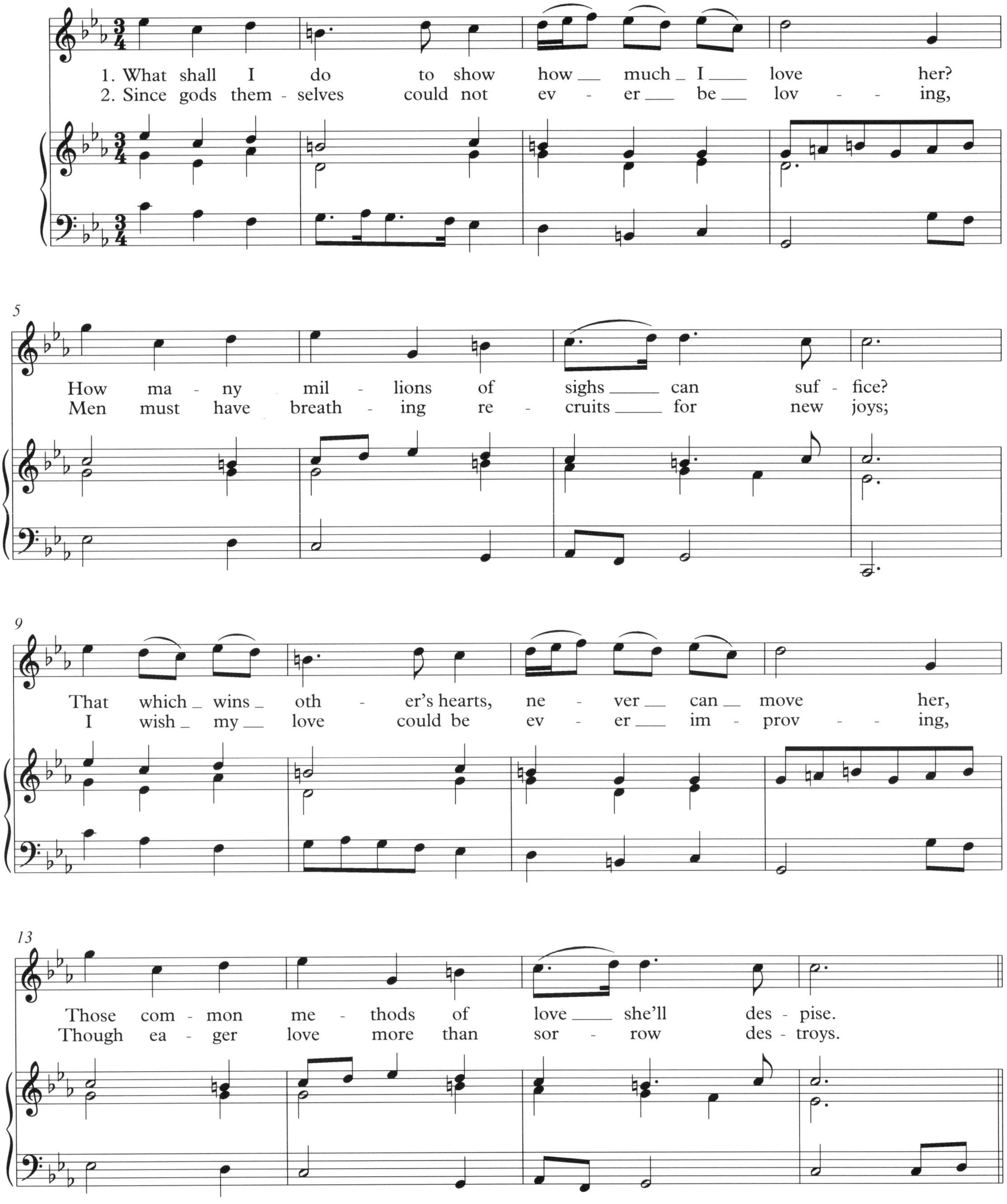
1. What shall I do to show how much I love her?
2. Since gods them - selves could not ev - er be lov - - ing,
5
How ma - ny mil - lions of sighs can suf - fice?
Men must have breath - ing re - cruits for new joys;
9
That which wins oth - er's hearts, ne - ver can move her,
I wish my love could be ev - er im - prov - - ing,
13
Those com - mon me - thods of love she'll des - pise.
Though ea - ger love more than sor - row des - troys.

If music be the food of love
First Version

Henry Heveningham (*c*.1651–1700)

Henry Purcell (1659–1695)

 range:

When Laura smiles

Anonymous
Philip Rosseter (1567/8–1623)

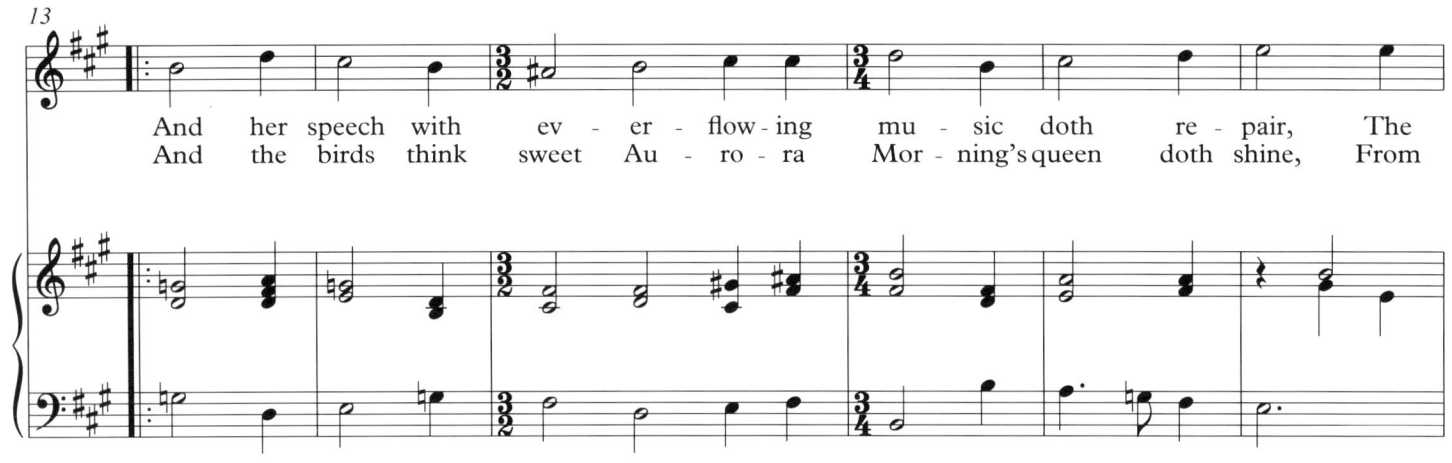

14

How beautiful are the feet
from *Messiah*

Charles Jennens (1700–1773)

George Frideric Handel (1685–1759)

range:

Larghetto

Un moto di gioja

My heart in confusion★

from *The Marriage of Figaro*

Lorenzo da Ponte (1749–1838)

Wolfgang Amadeus Mozart (1756–1791)

range:

★ English text © 1994 by Anne Ridler. Reproduced by permission of the translator.

range:

But Thou didst not leave His soul in hell

from *Messiah*

Charles Jennens (1700–1773)
George Frideric Handel (1685–1759)

Accompagnato
Recitative

He was cut off out of the land of the liv-ing;

for the trans-gres-sion of Thy peo-ple was He stri-cken.

Aria
Andante larghetto

But Thou didst not leave His soul in — hell,

19

range:

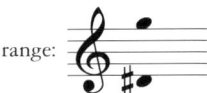

Behold and see if there be any sorrow

from *Messiah*

Charles Jennens (1700–1773)

George Frideric Handel (1685–1759)

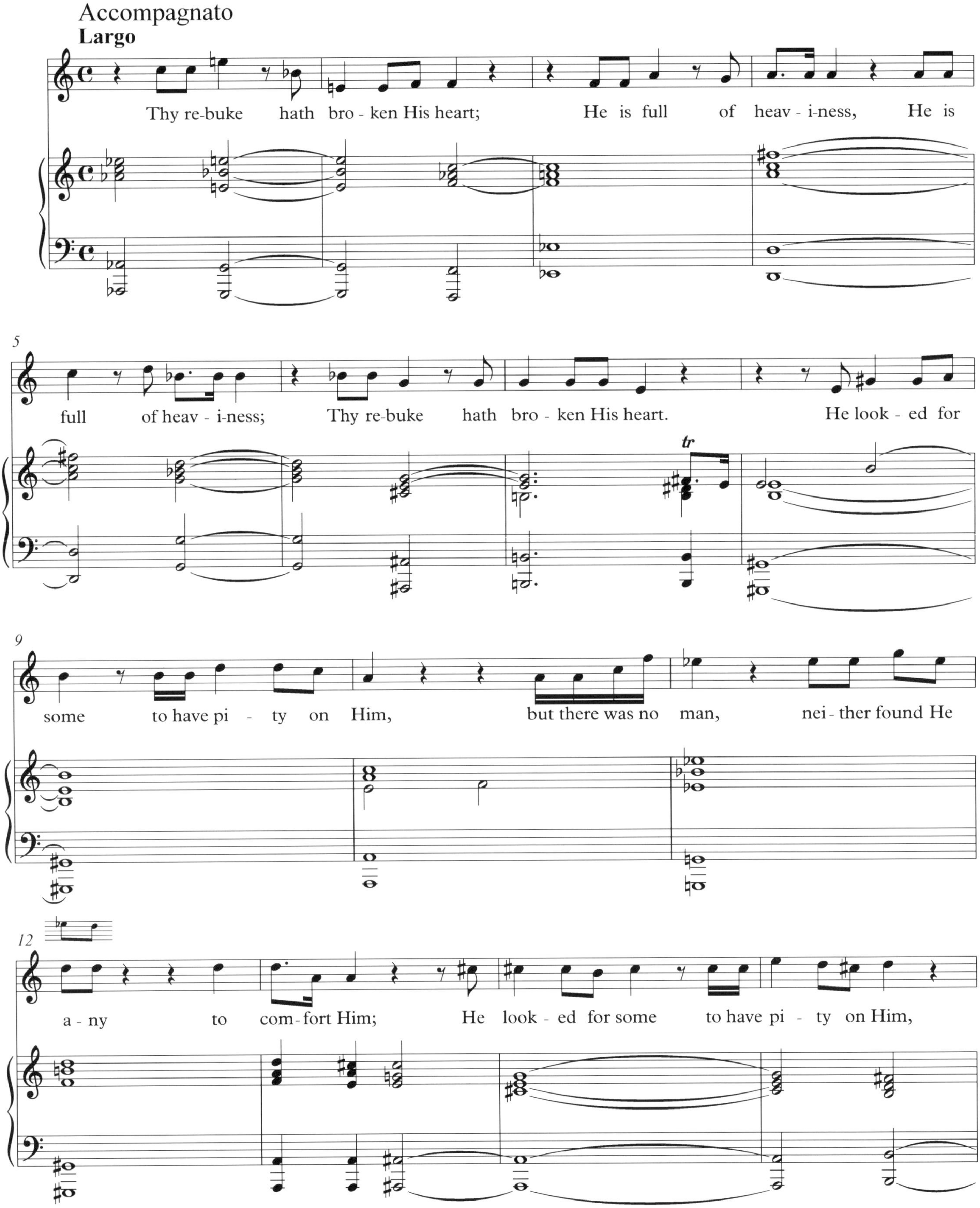
Accompagnato
Largo
Thy re-buke hath bro - ken His heart; He is full of heav - i-ness, He is
5
full of heav - i-ness; Thy re-buke hath bro - ken His heart. He look - ed for
tr
9
some to have pi - ty on Him, but there was no man, nei - ther found He
12
a - ny to com - fort Him; He look - ed for some to have pi - ty on Him,

An Epithalamium: Thrice happy lovers
from *The Fairy Queen*

Elkanah Settle (1648–1724)

Henry Purcell (1659–1695)

range:

Ich liebe dich

Karl Friedrich Wilhelm Herrosee (1764–1821)

Ludwig van Beethoven (1770–1827)

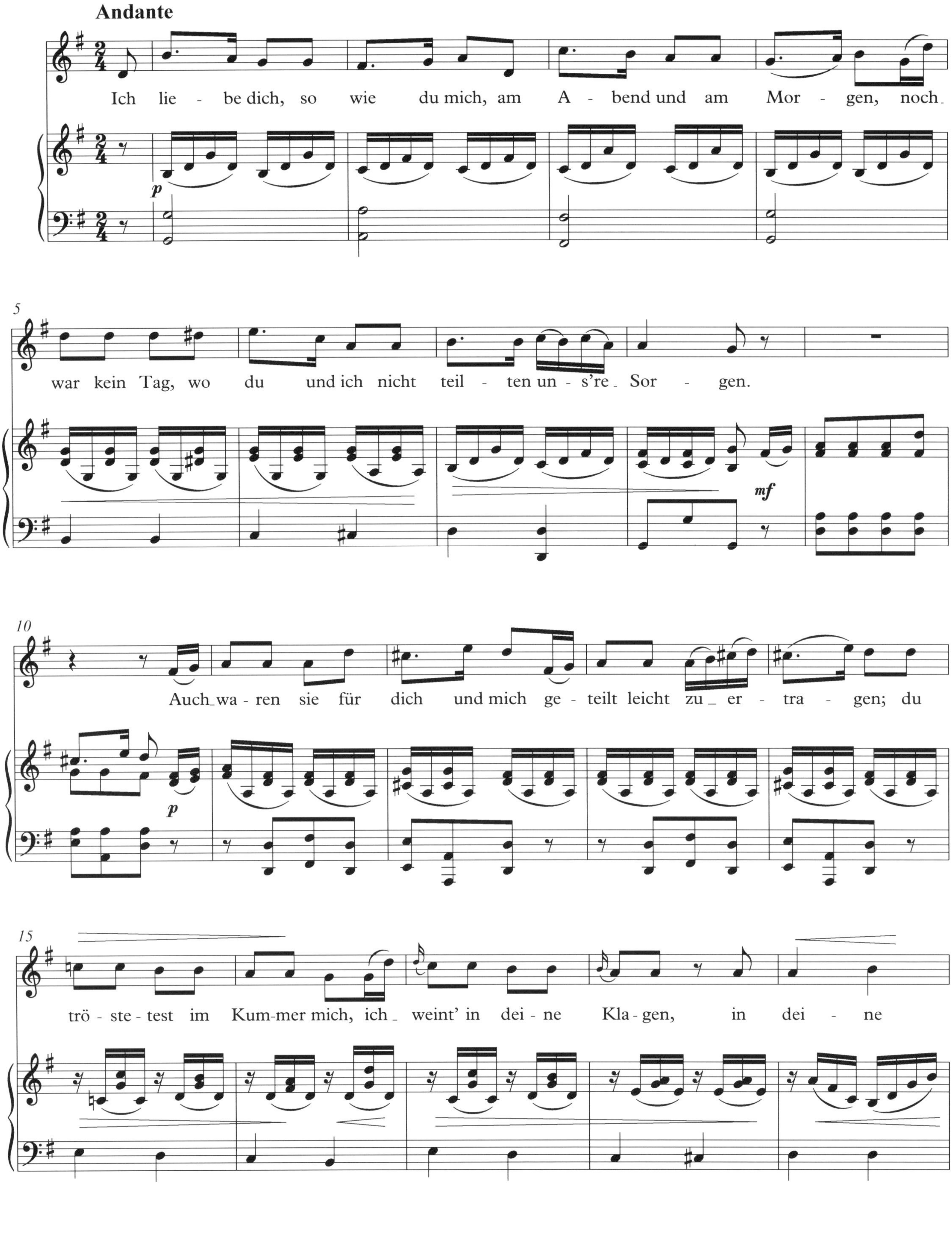

Feldeinsamkeit

Hermann Allmers (1821–1902)
Johannes Brahms (1833–1897)

O liebliche Wangen

Paul Fleming (1609–1640)
Johannes Brahms (1833–1897)

range:

Wiegenlied

Folksong from "Des Knaben Wunderhorn" (verse 1) /
Georg Scherer (1540–1605) (verse 2)

Johannes Brahms (1833–1897)

Scheiden und Meiden

Ludwig Uhland (1787–1862)
Johannes Brahms (1833–1897)

An den Frühling

Friedrich Schiller (1759–1805)
Franz Schubert (1797–1828)

range:

Mässig, heiter

1. Willkommen, schöner Jüngling! Du Wonne der Natur! Mit deinem Blumenkörbchen willkommen auf der Flur! Ei! ei! da bist ja wieder! und bist so lieb und schön! und freu'n wir uns so herzlich, entgegen dir zu geh'n und freu'n wir uns so herzlich, entgegen dir zu geh'n.

2. Denkst auch noch an mein Mädchen? Ei, Lieber, denke doch! dort liebte mich das Mädchen, und's Mädchen liebt mich noch. Für's Mädchen manches Blümchen erbat ich mir von dir, ich komm und bitte wieder, und du? du giebst es mir, ich komm und bitte wieder, und du? du giebst es mir.

An den Frühling

Friedrich Schiller (1759–1805)

Franz Schubert (1797–1828)

range:

Etwas geschwind

1. Will-kom-men, schö-ner Jüng-ling! du Won-ne der Na-tur! Mit dei-nem Blu-men-körb-chen, will-kom-men auf der Flur, will-kom-men
   auch noch an mein Mäd-chen? Ei, Lie-ber, den-ke doch! Dort lieb-te mich das Mäd-chen, und 's Mäd-chen liebt mich noch, und 's Mäd-chen
   -kom-men, schö-ner Jüng-ling! du Won-ne der Na-tur! Mit dei-nem Blu-men-körb-chen, will-kom-men auf der Flur, will-kom-men

range:

Die Forelle

Christian Friedrich Daniel Schubart (1739–1791)

Franz Schubert (1797–1828)

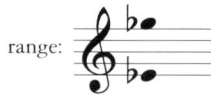

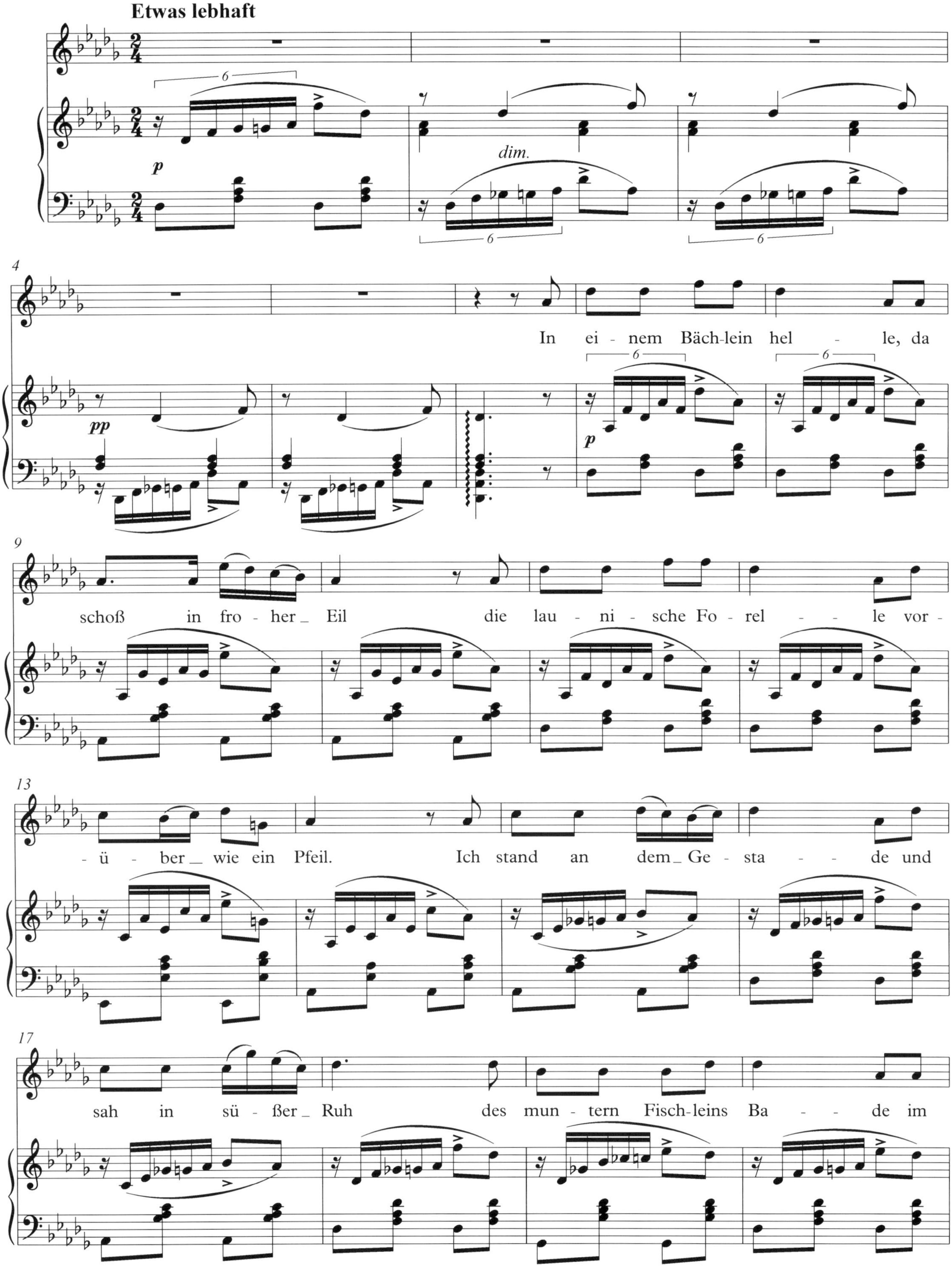
Etwas lebhaft
p
dim.
pp
In ei - nem Bäch-lein hel - le, da
schoß in fro - her_ Eil die lau - ni - sche Fo - rel - le vor -
- ü - ber_ wie ein Pfeil. Ich stand an dem_ Ge - sta - de und
sah in sü - ßer_ Ruh des mun - tern Fisch-leins Ba - de im

range:

Nachtviolen

Johann Mayrhofer (1787–1836)

Franz Schubert (1797–1828)

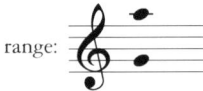

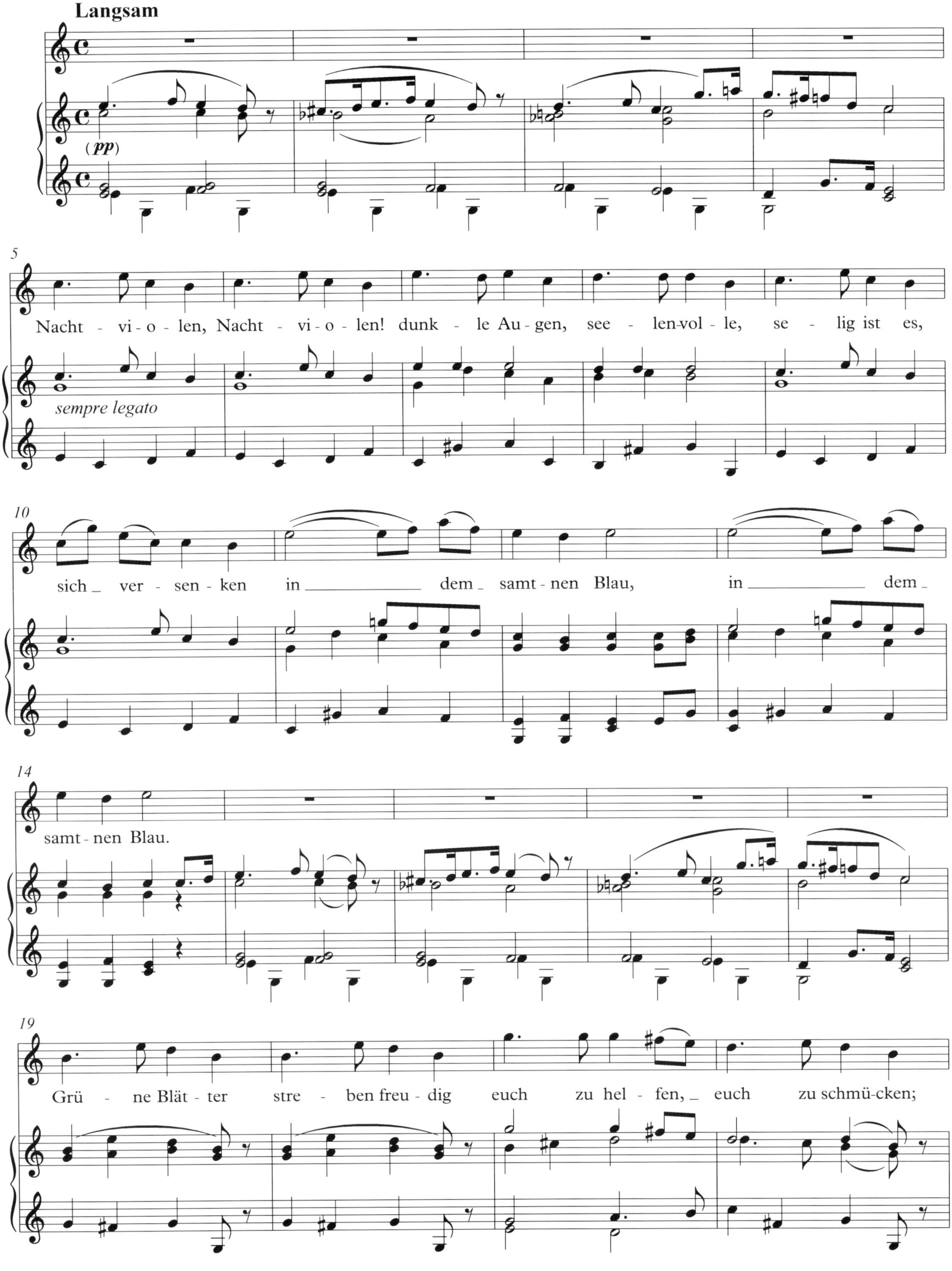
Langsam
(pp)
5
Nacht - vi - o - len, Nacht - vi - o - len! dunk - le Au - gen, see - len-vol - le, se - lig ist es,
sempre legato
10
sich _ ver - sen - ken in _ dem _ samt - nen Blau, in _ dem _
14
samt - nen Blau.
19
Grü - ne Blät - ter stre - ben freu - dig euch zu hel - fen, _ euch zu schmü - cken;

Frühlingsglaube

Ludwig Uhland (1787–1862)

Franz Schubert (1797–1828)

Ziemlich langsam

Die lin-den Lüf-te sind er-wacht, sie säu-seln und we-hen Tag und Nacht, sie schaf-fen an al-len En-den, an al-len En-den. O fri-scher Duft, o neu-er Klang, o neu-er Klang! Nun, ar-mes Her-ze,

range: 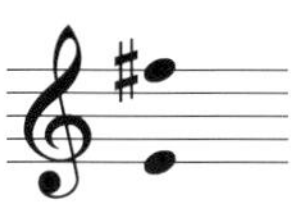

Mondnacht

Joseph von Eichendorff (1788–1857)

Robert Schumann (1810–1856)

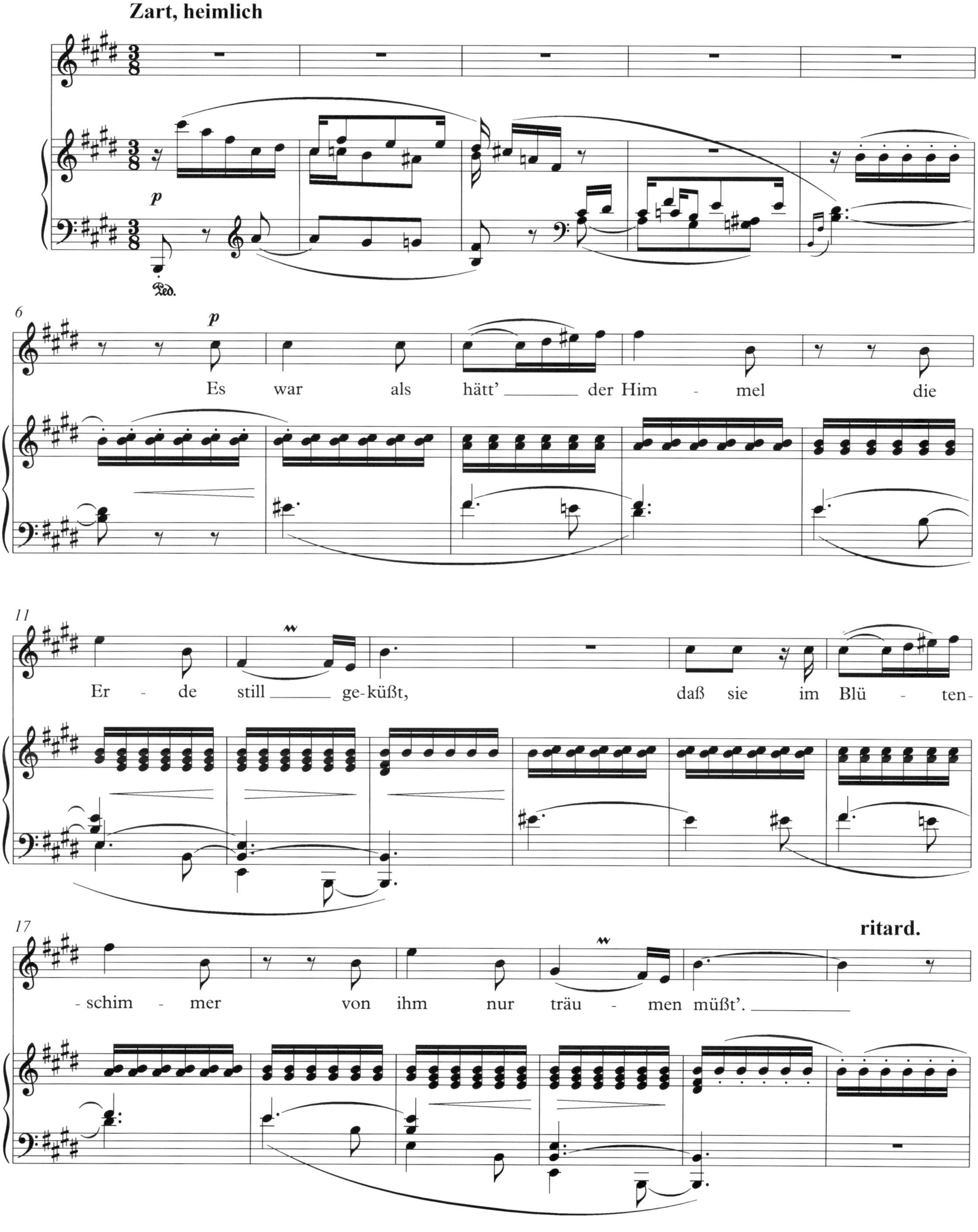
Zart, heimlich
p
Ped.
6
p
Es war als hätt' der Him - mel die
11
Er - de still ge-küßt, daß sie im Blü - ten-
17
ritard.
- schim - mer von ihm nur träu - men müßt'.

range:

Die Lotosblume

Heinrich Heine (1797–1856)

Robert Schumann (1810–1856)

Ziemlich langsam

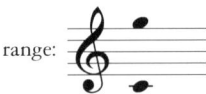

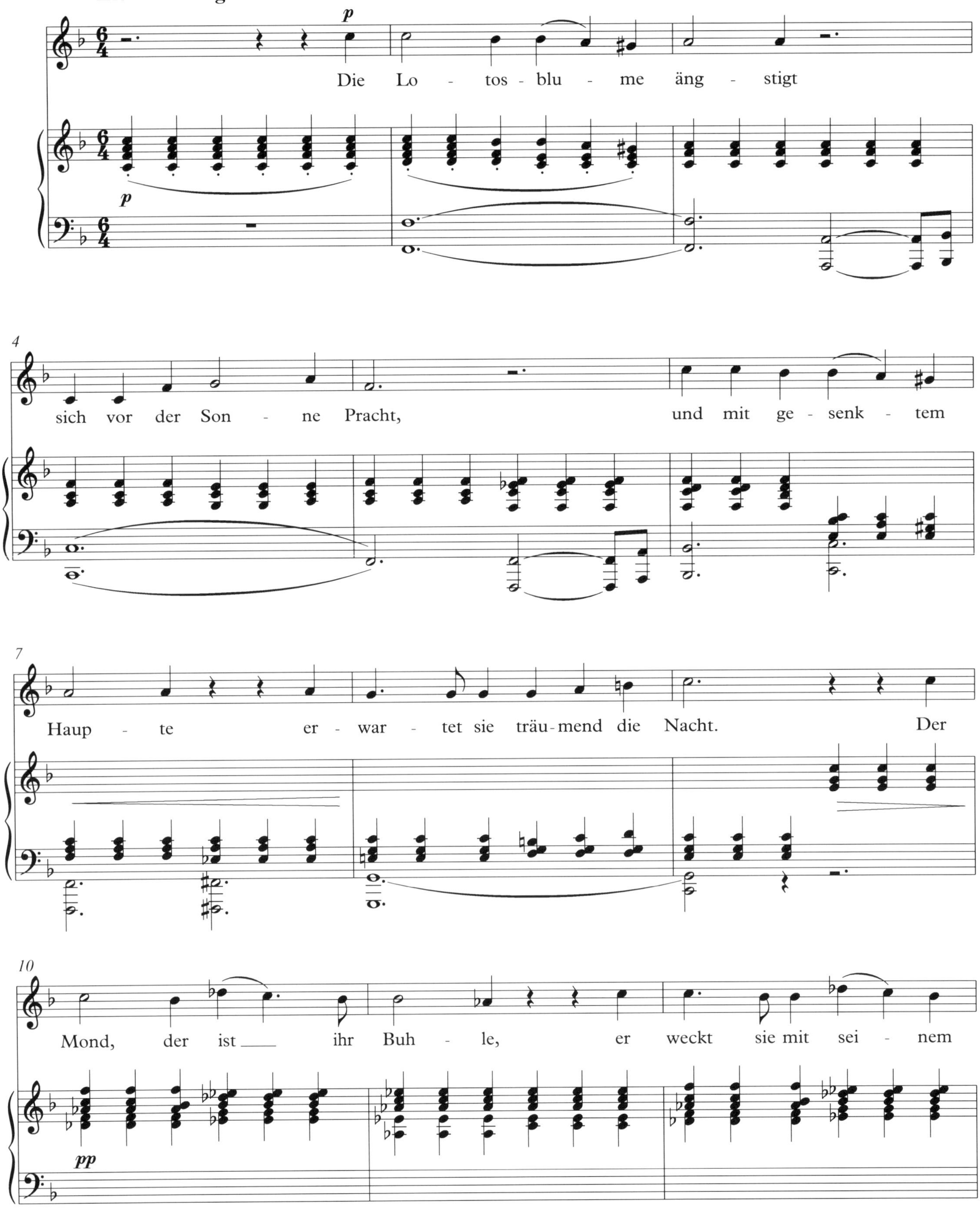
p
Die Lo - tos - blu - me äng - stigt
p
4
sich vor der Son - ne Pracht,
und mit ge - senk - tem
7
Haup - te er - war - tet sie träu - mend die Nacht.
Der
10
Mond, der ist ihr Buh - le,
er weckt sie mit sei - nem
pp

Il poveretto

Manfredo Maggioni
Giuseppe Verdi (1813–1901)

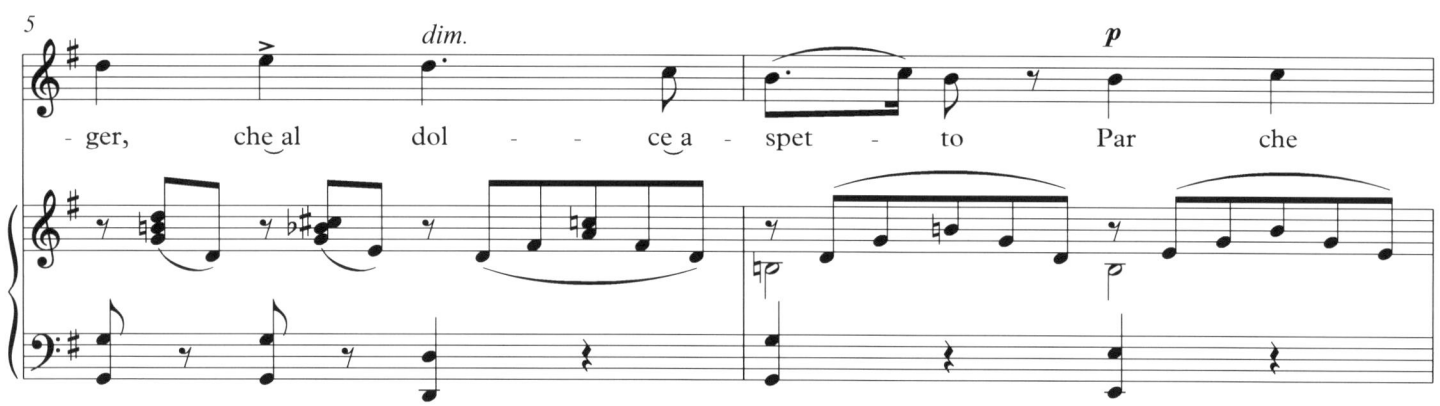

'A Vucchella

Gabriele d'Annunzio (1863–1938)

Francesco Paolo Tosti (1846–1916)

Allegretto moderato

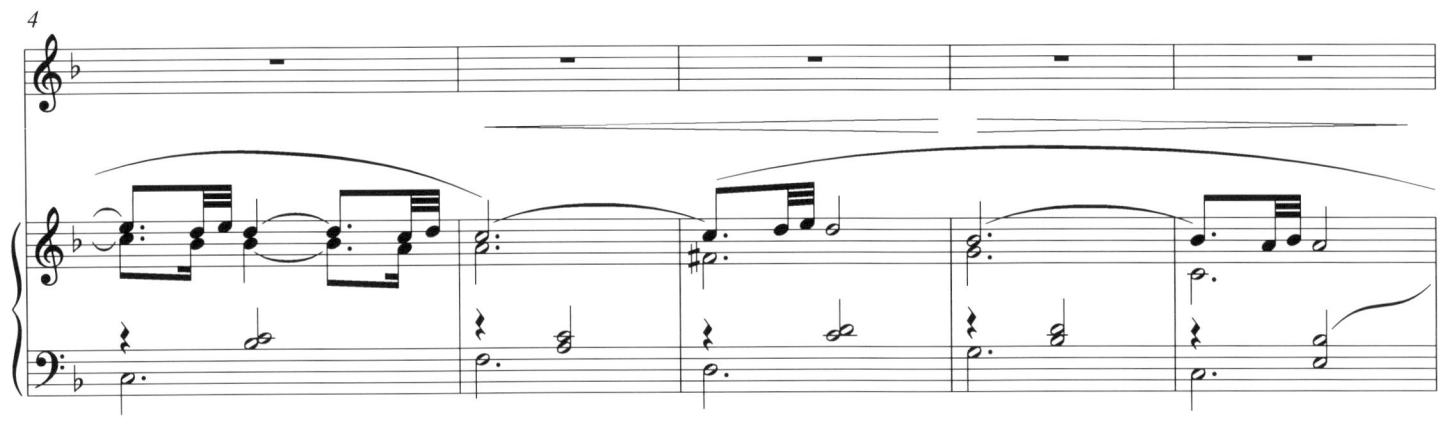

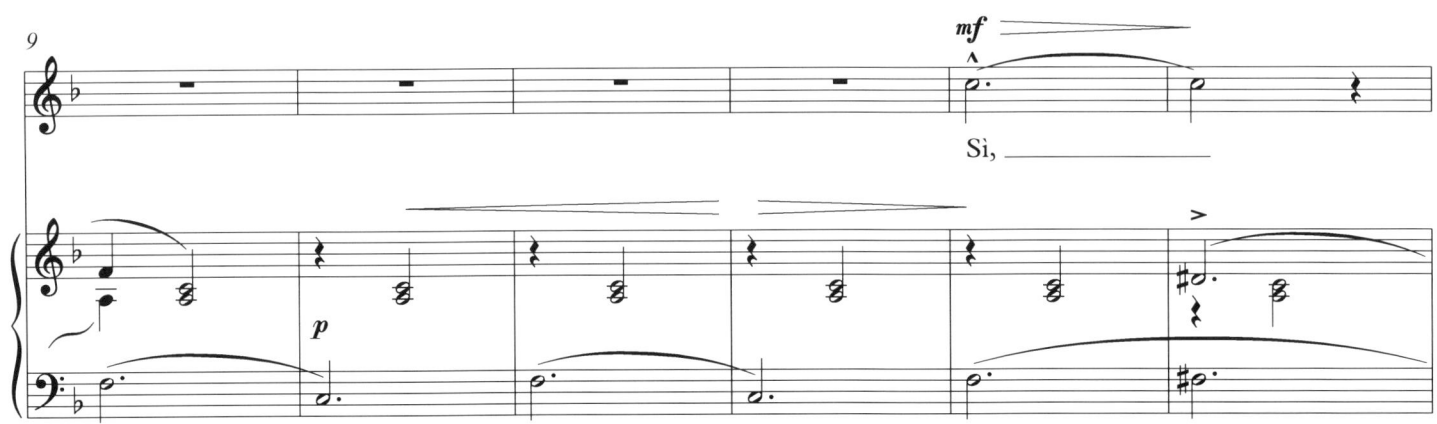

Si,

range:

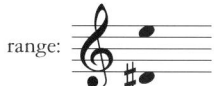

Der Musikant

Joseph von Eichendorff (1788–1857)

Hugo Wolf (1860–1903)

Sehr mässig

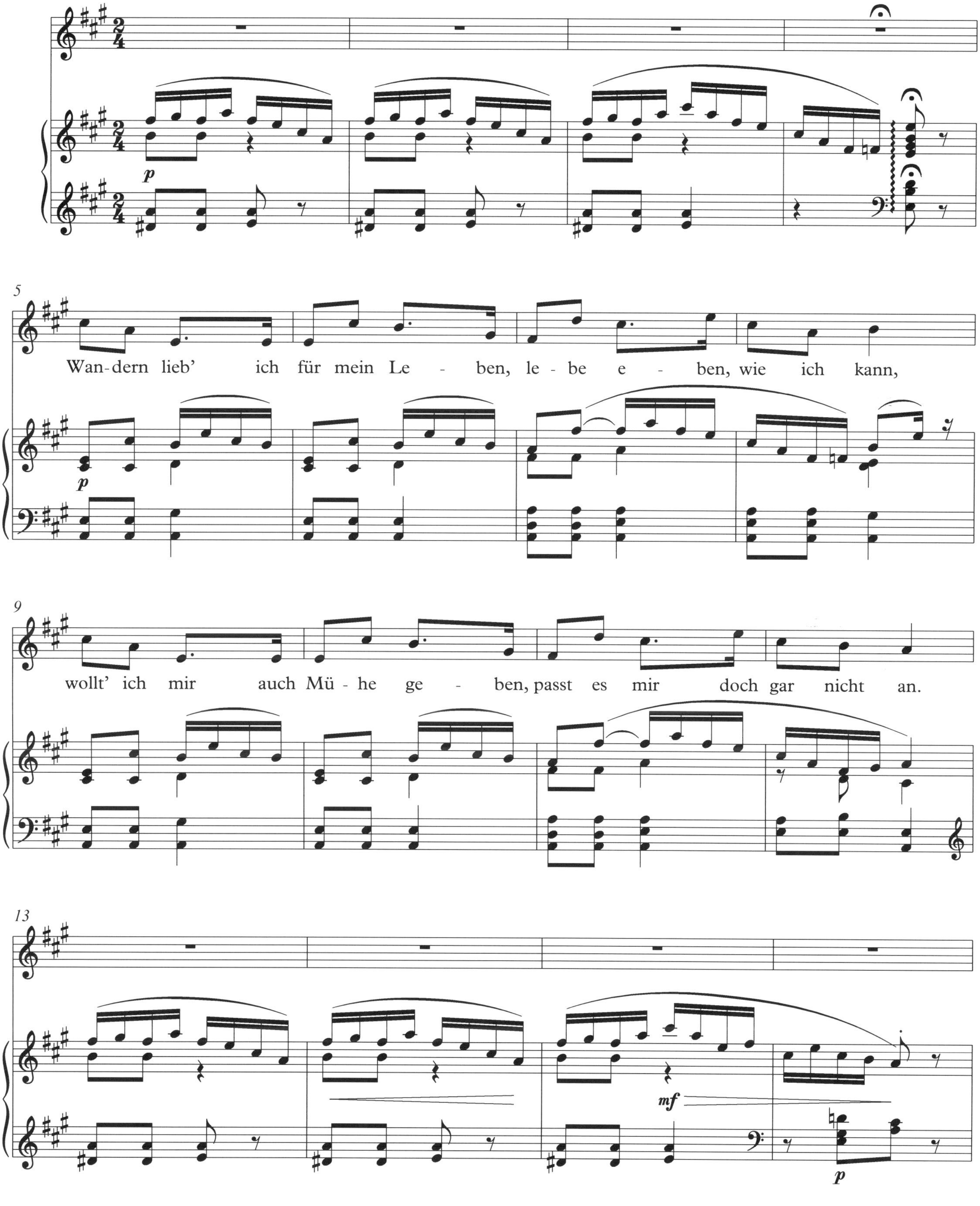
p
5
Wan-dern lieb' ich für mein Le - ben, le - be e - ben, wie ich kann,
p
9
wollt' ich mir auch Mü - he ge - ben, passt es mir doch gar nicht an.
13
mf
p

Der Gärtner

Eduard Mörike (1804–1875) — Hugo Wolf (1860–1903)

74

She had a letter from her love
from *Merrie England*

Basil Hood (1864–1917)   Edward German (1862–1936)

range:

range:

Is life a boon?

from *The Yeomen of the Guard*

W.S. Gilbert (1836–1911)

Arthur Sullivan (1842–1900)

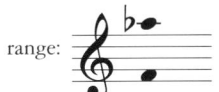

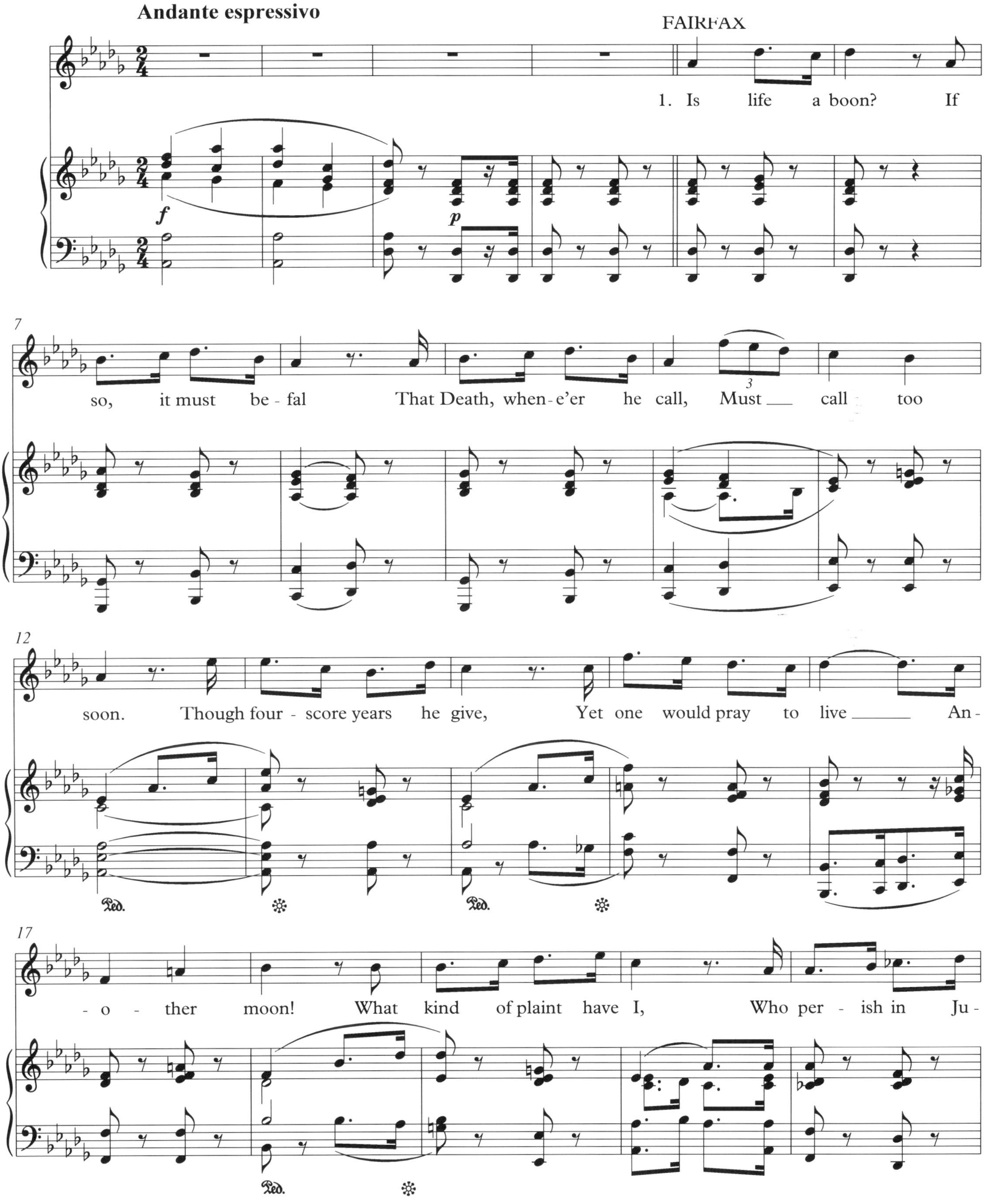

range:

The sun, whose rays are all ablaze

from *The Mikado*

W.S. Gilbert (1836–1911)

Arthur Sullivan (1842–1900)

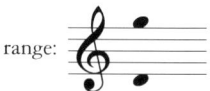

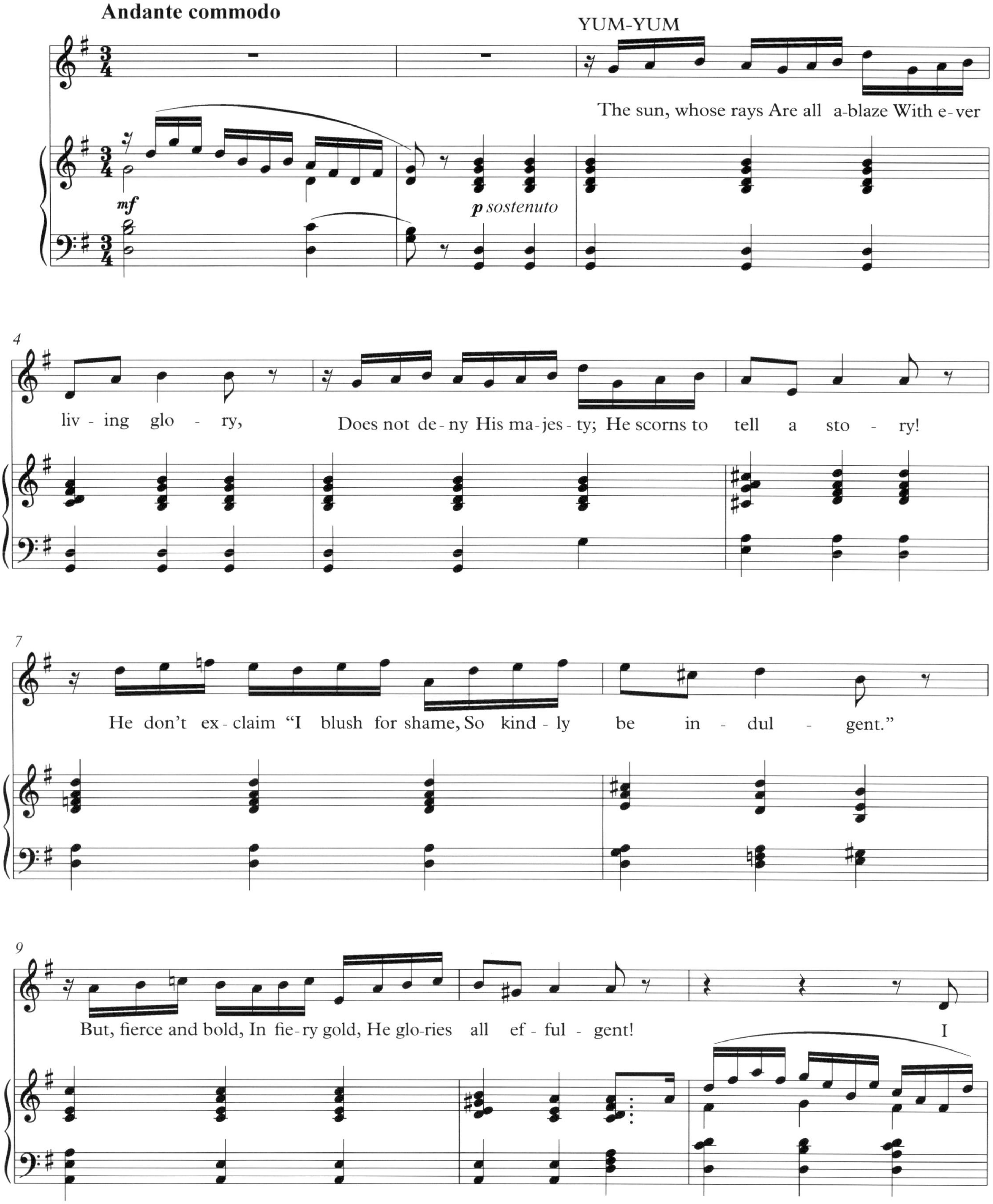
Andante commodo
YUM-YUM
The sun, whose rays Are all a-blaze With e-ver
mf
p sostenuto
4
liv - ing glo - ry, Does not de - ny His ma-jes - ty; He scorns to tell a sto - ry!
7
He don't ex - claim "I blush for shame, So kind - ly be in - dul - gent."
9
But, fierce and bold, In fie - ry gold, He glo-ries all ef - ful - gent! I